THIS NOTEBOOK BELONGS TO

_____

_____

DATE:___/___/_____

WHOEVER DOES NOT TAKE UP THEIR CROSS AND FOLLOW ME IS NOT WORTHY OF ME.
-MATTHEW 10:38

DATE:___/___/_____

I REMAIN CONFIDENT OF THIS: I WILL SEE THE GOODNESS OF THE LORD IN THE LAND
OF THE LIVING.
-PSALM 27:13

DATE:___/___/_____

The grace of the Lord Jesus Christ be with your spirit.
-Philemon 1:25

DATE:___/___/_____

Be strong and take heart, all you who hope in the Lord.
-Psalm 31:24

DATE:___/___/_____

COMMIT TO THE LORD WHATEVER YOU DO, AND HE WILL ESTABLISH YOUR PLANS.
-PROVERBS 16:3

DATE:___/___/____

But you, Lord, are a shield around me, my glory, the One who lifts my head high.
-Psalm 3:3

DATE:___/___/_____

LET YOUR GENTLENESS BE EVIDENT TO ALL. THE LORD IS NEAR.
-PHILIPPIANS 4:5

DATE:___/___/_____

PEACEMAKERS WHO SOW IN PEACE REAP A HARVEST OF RIGHTEOUSNESS.
-JAMES 3:18

DATE:___/___/_____

YOU ARE ALREADY CLEAN BECAUSE OF THE WORD I HAVE SPOKEN TO YOU.
-JOHN 15:3

DATE:____/____/_____

BUT LET JUSTICE ROLL ON LIKE A RIVER, RIGHTEOUSNESS LIKE A NEVER-FAILING
STREAM!
-AMOS 5:24

How much better to get wisdom than gold, to get insight rather than silver!
-Proverbs 16:16

_____
_____
_____
_____
_____
_____
_____
_____
_____
_____
_____
_____
_____
_____
_____
_____
_____
_____
_____
_____
_____
_____
_____
_____
_____
_____
_____
_____
_____

DATE:___/___/_____

For the word of the Lord is right and true; he is faithful in all he does.
-Psalm 33:4

DATE:___/___/_____

They replied, "Believe in the Lord Jesus, and you will be saved—you and your household."
-Acts 16:31

_____
_____
_____
_____
_____
_____
_____
_____
_____
_____
_____
_____
_____
_____
_____
_____
_____
_____
_____
_____
_____
_____
_____
_____
_____
_____
_____
_____

DATE:___/___/_____

DATE:___/___/_____

He gives strength to the weary and increases the power of the weak.
-Isaiah 40:29

DATE:____/____/_____

DO EVERYTHING IN LOVE.
-1 CORINTHIANS 16:14

DATE:___/___/_____

A PERVERSE PERSON STIRS UP CONFLICT, AND A GOSSIP SEPARATES CLOSE FRIENDS.
-PROVERBS 16:28

_____
_____
_____
_____
_____
_____
_____
_____
_____
_____
_____
_____
_____
_____
_____
_____
_____
_____
_____
_____
_____
_____
_____
_____
_____
_____
_____
_____

DATE:___/___/_____

SPEAK UP FOR THOSE WHO CANNOT SPEAK FOR THEMSELVES, FOR THE RIGHTS OF ALL WHO
ARE DESTITUTE.
-PROVERBS 31:8

DATE:___/___/_____

WHOEVER BELIEVES AND IS BAPTIZED WILL BE SAVED, BUT WHOEVER DOES NOT BELIEVE
WILL BE CONDEMNED.
-MARK 16:16

DATE:___/___/_____

BLESSED ARE THE PEACEMAKERS, FOR THEY WILL BE CALLED CHILDREN OF GOD.
-MATTHEW 5:9

DATE:____/____/_____

WHOEVER BELIEVES AND IS BAPTIZED WILL BE SAVED, BUT WHOEVER DOES NOT BELIEVE WILL BE CONDEMNED.
-MARK 16:16

_____
_____
_____
_____
_____
_____
_____
_____
_____
_____
_____
_____
_____
_____
_____
_____
_____
_____
_____
_____
_____
_____
_____
_____
_____
_____
_____
_____
_____
_____
_____
_____

DATE:___/___/_____

TWO ARE BETTER THAN ONE, BECAUSE THEY HAVE A GOOD RETURN FOR THEIR LABOR.
-ECCLESIASTES 4:9

DATE:___/___/_____

And every tongue acknowledge that Jesus Christ is Lord, to the glory of God
the Father.
-Philippians 2:11

DATE:___/___/_____

WAIT FOR THE LORD; BE STRONG AND TAKE HEART AND WAIT FOR THE LORD.
-PSALM 27:14

DATE:___/___/_____

HE SENT OUT HIS WORD AND HEALED THEM; HE RESCUED THEM FROM THE GRAVE.
-PSALM 107:20

DATE:___/___/____

WHOEVER WALKS IN INTEGRITY WALKS SECURELY, BUT WHOEVER TAKES CROOKED PATHS
WILL BE FOUND OUT.
-PROVERBS 10:9

DATE:___/___/_____

FEAR OF MAN WILL PROVE TO BE A SNARE, BUT WHOEVER TRUSTS IN THE LORD IS KEPT
SAFE.
-PROVERBS 29:25

_____
_____
_____
_____
_____
_____
_____
_____
_____
_____
_____
_____
_____
_____
_____
_____
_____
_____
_____
_____
_____
_____
_____
_____
_____
_____
_____
_____
_____

DATE:___/___/_____

DO NOT WITHHOLD YOUR MERCY FROM ME, LORD; MAY YOUR LOVE AND FAITHFULNESS ALWAYS PROTECT ME.
-PSALM 40:11

DATE:___/___/_____

WHOEVER CONCEALS HATRED WITH LYING LIPS AND SPREADS SLANDER IS A FOOL.
-PROVERBS 10:18

DATE:___/___/____

GRACIOUS WORDS ARE A HONEYCOMB, SWEET TO THE SOUL AND HEALING TO THE BONES.
-PROVERBS 16:24

DATE:___/___/_____

WHO IS IT THAT OVERCOMES THE WORLD? ONLY THE ONE WHO BELIEVES THAT JESUS IS
THE SON OF GOD.
-1 JOHN 5:5

DATE:___/___/____

For no word from God will ever fail.
-Luke 1:37

DATE:___/___/_____

SPEAK UP FOR THOSE WHO CANNOT SPEAK FOR THEMSELVES, FOR THE RIGHTS OF ALL WHO
ARE DESTITUTE.
-PROVERBS 31:8

DATE:___/___/_____

THOSE WHOM I LOVE I REBUKE AND DISCIPLINE. SO BE EARNEST AND REPENT.
-REVELATION 3:19

DATE:___/___/_____

DO NOT BE MISLED: "BAD COMPANY CORRUPTS GOOD CHARACTER."
-1 CORINTHIANS 15:33

DATE:___/___/____

Then you will call on me and come and pray to me, and I will listen to you.
-Jeremiah 29:12

DATE:___/___/_____

WHOEVER IS PATIENT HAS GREAT UNDERSTANDING, BUT ONE WHO IS QUICK-TEMPERED
DISPLAYS FOLLY.
-PROVERBS 14:29

DATE:___/___/____

DO NOT BE MISLED: "BAD COMPANY CORRUPTS GOOD CHARACTER."
-1 CORINTHIANS 15:33

DATE:___/___/_____

GOD "WILL REPAY EACH PERSON ACCORDING TO WHAT THEY HAVE DONE."
-ROMANS 2:6

DATE:____/____/_____

Surely the Sovereign Lord does nothing without revealing his plan to his servants the prophets.
-Amos 3:7

_____
_____
_____
_____
_____
_____
_____
_____
_____
_____
_____
_____
_____
_____
_____
_____
_____
_____
_____
_____
_____
_____
_____
_____
_____
_____
_____
_____
_____
_____

DATE:___/___/_____

HOPE DEFERRED MAKES THE HEART SICK, BUT A LONGING FULFILLED IS A TREE OF LIFE.
-PROVERBS 13:12

DATE:___/___/_____

I HAVE NO GREATER JOY THAN TO HEAR THAT MY CHILDREN ARE WALKING IN THE
TRUTH.
-3 JOHN 1:4

DATE:___/___/_____

WAIT FOR THE LORD; BE STRONG AND TAKE HEART AND WAIT FOR THE LORD.
-PSALM 27:14

DATE:___/___/____

A NEW COMMAND I GIVE YOU: LOVE ONE ANOTHER. AS I HAVE LOVED YOU, SO YOU
MUST LOVE ONE ANOTHER.
-JOHN 13:34

DATE:___/___/____

WHAT, THEN, SHALL WE SAY IN RESPONSE TO THESE THINGS? IF GOD IS FOR US, WHO
CAN BE AGAINST US?
-ROMANS 8:31

_____
_____
_____
_____
_____
_____
_____
_____
_____
_____
_____
_____
_____
_____
_____
_____
_____
_____
_____
_____
_____
_____
_____
_____
_____
_____
_____
_____
_____
_____

DATE:___/___/_____

COME, LET US BOW DOWN IN WORSHIP, LET US KNEEL BEFORE THE LORD OUR MAKER.
-PSALM 95:6

DATE:___/___/____

A MEDIATOR, HOWEVER, IMPLIES MORE THAN ONE PARTY; BUT GOD IS ONE.
-GALATIANS 3:20

DATE:___/___/_____

FOOLS FIND NO PLEASURE IN UNDERSTANDING BUT DELIGHT IN AIRING THEIR OWN
OPINIONS.
-PROVERBS 18:2

_____
_____
_____
_____
_____
_____
_____
_____
_____
_____
_____
_____
_____
_____
_____
_____
_____
_____
_____
_____
_____
_____
_____
_____
_____
_____
_____
_____
_____

DATE:___/___/_____

For no word from God will ever fail.
-Luke 1:37

DATE:___/___/_____

WHOEVER FINDS THEIR LIFE WILL LOSE IT, AND WHOEVER LOSES THEIR LIFE FOR MY SAKE
WILL FIND IT.
-MATTHEW 10:39

DATE:___/___/____

THE WICKED BORROW AND DO NOT REPAY, BUT THE RIGHTEOUS GIVE GENEROUSLY.
-PSALM 37:21

DATE:___/___/_____

WATCH OUT THAT YOU DO NOT LOSE WHAT WE HAVE WORKED FOR, BUT THAT YOU MAY BE
REWARDED FULLY.
-2 JOHN 1:8

DATE:___/___/____

Come to me, all you who are weary and burdened, and I will give you rest.
-Matthew 11:28

DATE:___/___/_____

THOSE WHOM I LOVE I REBUKE AND DISCIPLINE. SO BE EARNEST AND REPENT.
-REVELATION 3:19

DATE:___/___/_____

Even fools are thought wise if they keep silent, and discerning if they hold
their tongues.
-Proverbs 17:28

DATE:____/____/_____

Flesh gives birth to flesh, but the Spirit gives birth to spirit.
-John 3:6

DATE:___/___/_____

I HAVE NO GREATER JOY THAN TO HEAR THAT MY CHILDREN ARE WALKING IN THE
TRUTH.
-3 JOHN 1:4

DATE:____/____/_____

HERE IS A TRUSTWORTHY SAYING: IF WE DIED WITH HIM, WE WILL ALSO LIVE WITH HIM.
-2 TIMOTHY 2:11

DATE:___/___/_____

The wise in heart accept commands, but a chattering fool comes to ruin.
-Proverbs 10:8

DATE:___/___/_____

A FRIEND LOVES AT ALL TIMES, AND A BROTHER IS BORN FOR A TIME OF ADVERSITY.
-PROVERBS 17:17

DATE:___/___/_____

PUT ON THE FULL ARMOR OF GOD, SO THAT YOU CAN TAKE YOUR STAND AGAINST THE
DEVIL'S SCHEMES.
-EPHESIANS 6:11

DATE:___/___/____

Be exalted, O God, above the heavens; let your glory be over all the earth.
-PSALM 108:5

DATE:___/___/_____

BLESSED ARE THOSE WHO KEEP HIS STATUTES AND SEEK HIM WITH ALL THEIR HEART.
-PSALM 119:2

DATE:___/___/_____

SO I SAY, WALK BY THE SPIRIT, AND YOU WILL NOT GRATIFY THE DESIRES OF THE FLESH.
-GALATIANS 5:16

DATE:____/____/_____

DATE:___/___/_____

SHOW ME YOUR WAYS, LORD, TEACH ME YOUR PATHS.
-PSALM 25:4

DATE:___/___/_____

A FRIEND LOVES AT ALL TIMES, AND A BROTHER IS BORN FOR A TIME OF ADVERSITY.
-PROVERBS 17:17

DATE:___/___/____

GIVE TO EVERYONE WHO ASKS YOU, AND IF ANYONE TAKES WHAT BELONGS TO YOU, DO
NOT DEMAND IT BACK.
-LUKE 6:30

DATE:___/___/_____

THE LIONS MAY GROW WEAK AND HUNGRY, BUT THOSE WHO SEEK THE LORD LACK NO
GOOD THING.
-PSALM 34:10

Date:___/___/_____

Do not withhold your mercy from me, Lord; may your love and faithfulness always protect me.
-Psalm 40:11

DATE:___/___/____

DO NOT TURN TO THE RIGHT OR THE LEFT; KEEP YOUR FOOT FROM EVIL.
-PROVERBS 4:27

PRODUCE FRUIT IN KEEPING WITH REPENTANCE.
-MATTHEW 3:8

DATE:___/___/____

I FELL TO THE GROUND AND HEARD A VOICE SAY TO ME, 'SAUL! SAUL! WHY DO YOU
PERSECUTE ME?'
-ACTS 22:7

DATE:___/___/_____

WHEN PRIDE COMES, THEN COMES DISGRACE, BUT WITH HUMILITY COMES WISDOM.
-PROVERBS 11:2

DATE:___/___/____

A PERSON'S RICHES MAY RANSOM THEIR LIFE, BUT THE POOR CANNOT RESPOND TO
THREATENING REBUKES.
-PROVERBS 13:8

DATE:___/___/_____

DEAR CHILDREN, KEEP YOURSELVES FROM IDOLS.
-1 JOHN 5:21

DATE:___/___/_____

IN FACT, EVERYONE WHO WANTS TO LIVE A GODLY LIFE IN CHRIST JESUS WILL BE
PERSECUTED.
-2 TIMOTHY 3:12

DATE:___/___/_____

AND IF WE KNOW THAT HE HEARS US—WHATEVER WE ASK—WE KNOW THAT WE HAVE
WHAT WE ASKED OF HIM.
-1 JOHN 5:15

DATE:___/___/_____

He who finds a wife finds what is good and receives favor from the Lord.
-Proverbs 18:22

DATE:___/___/_____

THE PRUDENT SEE DANGER AND TAKE REFUGE, BUT THE SIMPLE KEEP GOING AND PAY
THE PENALTY.
-PROVERBS 27:12

DATE:___/___/_____

PRIDE BRINGS A PERSON LOW, BUT THE LOWLY IN SPIRIT GAIN HONOR.
-PROVERBS 29:23

No one who denies the Son has the Father; whoever acknowledges the Son has the Father also.
-1 John 2:23

DATE:___/___/_____

GLORY TO GOD IN THE HIGHEST HEAVEN, AND ON EARTH PEACE TO THOSE ON WHOM HIS FAVOR RESTS.
-LUKE 2:14

DATE:___/___/_____

MY SON, IF YOUR HEART IS WISE, THEN MY HEART WILL BE GLAD INDEED.
-PROVERBS 23:15

DATE:___/___/____

FOR SIN SHALL NO LONGER BE YOUR MASTER, BECAUSE YOU ARE NOT UNDER THE LAW,
BUT UNDER GRACE.
-ROMANS 6:14

DATE:___/___/_____

WHAT A PERSON DESIRES IS UNFAILING LOVE; BETTER TO BE POOR THAN A LIAR.
-PROVERBS 19:22

DATE:___/___/____

WHOM HAVE I IN HEAVEN BUT YOU? AND EARTH HAS NOTHING I DESIRE BESIDES YOU.
-PSALM 73:25

DATE:___/___/_____

IN YOUR RELATIONSHIPS WITH ONE ANOTHER, HAVE THE SAME MINDSET AS CHRIST JESUS.
-PHILIPPIANS 2:5

DATE:___/___/____

GIVE PROPER RECOGNITION TO THOSE WIDOWS WHO ARE REALLY IN NEED.
-1 TIMOTHY 5:3

DATE:___/___/_____

EVEN FOOLS ARE THOUGHT WISE IF THEY KEEP SILENT, AND DISCERNING IF THEY HOLD
THEIR TONGUES.
-PROVERBS 17:28

DATE:___/___/_____

PRAISE THE LORD. BLESSED ARE THOSE WHO FEAR THE LORD, WHO FIND GREAT DELIGHT IN HIS COMMANDS.
-PSALM 112:1

DATE:___/___/_____

Jesus answered, "My teaching is not my own. It comes from the one who sent me."

-John 7:16

DATE:___/___/____

THE LORD MAKES FIRM THE STEPS OF THE ONE WHO DELIGHTS IN HIM.
-PSALM 37:23

DATE:___/___/_____

I WILL GIVE THANKS TO YOU, LORD, WITH ALL MY HEART; I WILL TELL OF ALL YOUR
WONDERFUL DEEDS.
-PSALM 9:1

DATE:___/___/_____

So that I may come to you with joy, by God's will, and in your company be
refreshed.
-Romans 15:32

_____
_____
_____
_____
_____
_____
_____
_____
_____
_____
_____
_____
_____
_____
_____
_____
_____
_____
_____
_____
_____
_____
_____
_____
_____
_____
_____
_____

DATE:___/___/_____

BETTER A PATIENT PERSON THAN A WARRIOR, ONE WITH SELF-CONTROL THAN ONE WHO
TAKES A CITY.
-PROVERBS 16:32

DATE:___/___/____

Praise the Lord, my soul; all my inmost being, praise his holy name.
-Psalm 103:1

DATE:___/___/_____

I AM COMING SOON. HOLD ON TO WHAT YOU HAVE, SO THAT NO ONE WILL TAKE YOUR CROWN.
-REVELATION 3:11

DATE:___/___/_____

ACCEPT THE ONE WHOSE FAITH IS WEAK, WITHOUT QUARRELING OVER DISPUTABLE
MATTERS.
-ROMANS 14:1

DATE:___/___/_____

AS THE DEER PANTS FOR STREAMS OF WATER, SO MY SOUL PANTS FOR YOU, MY GOD.
-PSALM 42:1

DATE:___/___/_____

BETTER A PATIENT PERSON THAN A WARRIOR, ONE WITH SELF-CONTROL THAN ONE WHO
TAKES A CITY.
-PROVERBS 16:32

DATE:___/___/_____

ALL DAY LONG HE CRAVES FOR MORE, BUT THE RIGHTEOUS GIVE WITHOUT SPARING.
-PROVERBS 21:26

DATE:___/___/_____

THE LORD MAKES FIRM THE STEPS OF THE ONE WHO DELIGHTS IN HIM.
-PSALM 37:23

DATE:___/___/_____

MY SON, KEEP YOUR FATHER'S COMMAND AND DO NOT FORSAKE YOUR MOTHER'S
TEACHING.
-PROVERBS 6:20

DATE:___/___/____

For he satisfies the thirsty and fills the hungry with good things.
-Psalm 107:9

DATE:___/___/_____

BUT I TELL YOU, LOVE YOUR ENEMIES AND PRAY FOR THOSE WHO PERSECUTE YOU.
-MATTHEW 5:44

Rejoice in the Lord always. I will say it again: Rejoice!
-Philippians 4:4

_____
_____
_____
_____
_____
_____
_____
_____
_____
_____
_____
_____
_____
_____
_____
_____
_____
_____
_____
_____
_____
_____
_____
_____
_____
_____
_____
_____
_____

GOD IS OUR REFUGE AND STRENGTH, AN EVER-PRESENT HELP IN TROUBLE.

-Psalm 46:1

Made in the USA
Monee, IL
27 April 2022

95555316R00063